To Jeff – Thank you for inspiring my love of the saguaro. Lisa Rose

For Mum and Dad, Stuart, Matt, and Lizzy. EG

SEÑOR SAGUARO
King of the Desert

By Lisa Rose
Illustrator Emma Graham

the little fig ®
www.thelittlefig.com

Sip Sip Sip!

Señor Saguaro
startled. "Qué pasa?
Who's waking me up
at this hora de
la noche?"

"Pardon, Señor. I want
to dine on your
fine nectar."

"Dine? On me?
How *dare* you!"

"I am King of the Desert! Not even a hundred years in the sol caliente with agua poco could prevent me from becoming GRANDE!"

Bat slurped. "That's why I'm here. Your nectar is of superb quality."

"El mejor nectar in the Southwest!"

"Yes, my friend." Bat agreed.

"Friend?!" Señor snorted. "How can your moonlit dining make you mi amigo?"

"Look at my mouth. It is covered with pollen dust. As I drink from this luscious flower, some of the pollen clings to my mouth. When I sip again, this pollen falls into the other blossoms."

"Ah!" said Señor. "So, this makes more flor lucioso?"

Bat took another sip. "Lucious and beautiful."

"Bueno, amigo."

"Qué pasa?" asked Señor. "Who's making that racket?"

"It's me. Just building a little home for me and the missus."

"What?" roared Señor. "La hacienda? In me?!"

tap Tap TAP!

"How *dare* you! *I* am King of the Desert!

Not even a hundred years in the sol caliente with agua poco could prevent *me* from becoming *GRANDE!*"

"You are very big," said Woodpecker. "That is why I chose you to keep my family safe and shaded. I will make a hole..."

"Un hoyo! That sounds painful!"

"It won't hurt you. You'll form a tough lining."

"How do you
know so much?"
asked Señor.

"I have a big brain,
my friend."

"How does your
cerebro grande
make us amigos?"

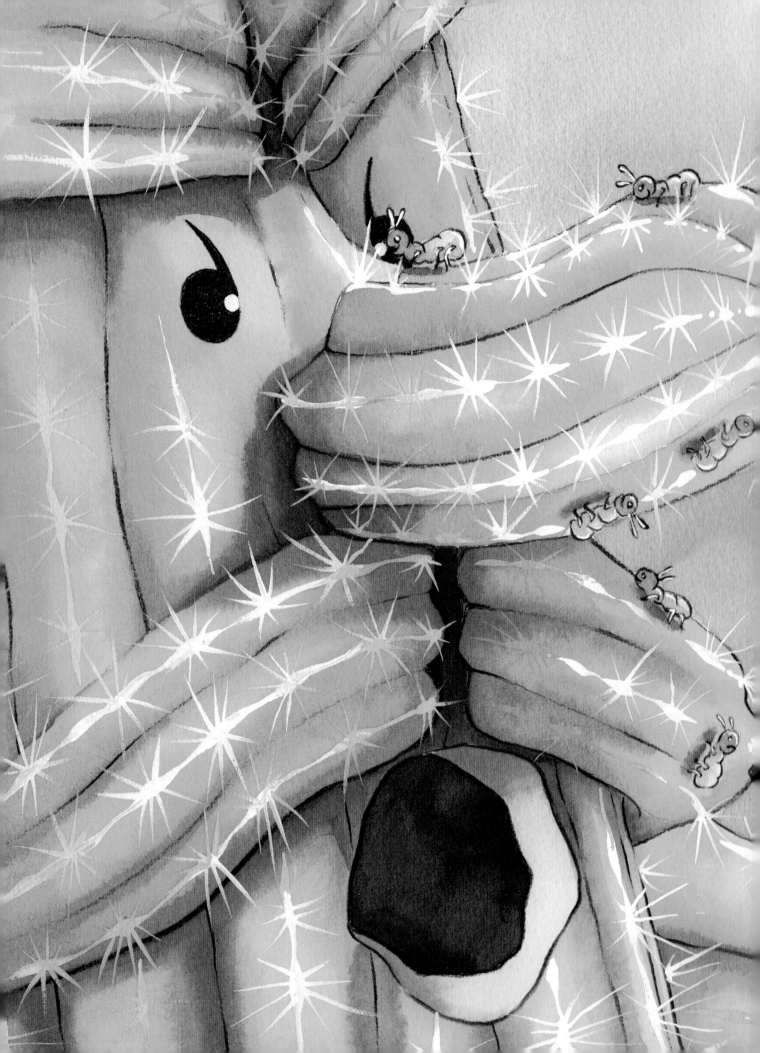

"I know enough to eat these pesky insects. The ones that can make you sick."

Senor shivered. "Those really bug me."

"What could be friendlier than the missus, me, and all our chicks eating them up and keeping you healthy?"

"Bueno, amigo."

"Qué pasa?" asked Señor. "Who is munching my fruit?"

"This is the sweetest thing I've ever tasted! I'm gonna gather all I can and stuff my home with them."

munch Munch MUNCH!

"How *dare* you! *I* am King of the Desert! Not even a hundred years in the sol caliente with agua poco could prevent *me* from becoming *GRANDE*!"

"I say you are King of the Dessert," laughed Pack Rat. "Your fruit is the juiciest!"

"Not dessert. *Desert*, you rodent!"

Munch!!

Crunch!!

"As you say, my friend. Your fruit is so good I'm gonna gather all I can..."

"I heard you the first time. Tell me how eating mi fruta makes you mi amigo?"

"I will take your fruit so deep into my home, even I will forget where I buried it. The seeds inside the fruit will take root."

"Fantástico!" said Señor.

"And I will do something else too," said Pack Rat.

"When I eat your fruit, I can't digest the seeds. Every time I drop my skinny poop pellets, I scatter your seeds. My poop is fertilizer and will help your seeds grow. Your offspring will sprout all across the desert."

"So, you will make sure I am always King of the Desert with many royal descendants?" asked Señor.

"I will," said Pack Rat.

"Bueno!"

"Sip, tap, and munch away!
Muchas gracias, mi amigos!"

Long live the King of the Desert!

Fun Facts

- The saguaro is a tree-like cactus that is native to the Southwest United States. Saguaros can live to be almost 200 years old! That is older than any human.

- A full-grown saguaro can grow to be 40-50 feet tall, about the same size as a two-story house.

- Saguaros can weigh over 4,000 pounds, the average weight of two cars!

- Saguaros grows very slowly. After 10 years, a saguaro is only around one-and-a-half inches tall.

- Saguaro flowers bloom for less than one day. They open at night and bloom throughout the morning.

- A single saguaro fruit is the size of a large strawberry. Each fruit has over 1,000 tiny black seeds—more seeds than three pumpkins!

- Pack rats don't drink water, but they do urinate. They pee in their nests! When the urine dries it crystalizes and preserves objects in the nests for thousands of years. Archeologists can learn about Ice Age environments because of pack rat pee.